"Anthony Carter tells the story of his remarkable life with humility and wonder that has lessons for us all. He faced the indignities and suffering of the world with an open heart and courage rooted in deep faith."

—Tania Tetlow, President, Fordham University

"Anthony Carter's *This I Know* is a story of passion, faith, love, and, above all, sincerity. While reading, I found myself laughing, crying, and reflecting a lot on family, what it means to give and receive love, and how our diversity makes us all stronger people. This is the writing of a man who cares deeply and truly about others, and I know you will be moved and changed for the better in feeling that care in his writing. This isn't just a story well told; it's a life fully lived, and bravely shared. If Wisdom were writing in his diary while listening to some djembe drums, this would be it."

—Dr. Richie Diaz, EdD, Principal, Cathedral Preparatory School and Seminary in New York

"From the heart of the South Bronx to the pinnacle of corporate America, Anthony Carter's life story is a testament to the power of an indomitable spirit, extraordinary abilities, and faith in God. For more than fifty years, he has been one of the most extraordinary people I know. Now, through this book of wisdom, I invite you to know him too."

—Ted Shaw, Former Director Counsel of the NAACP Legal Defense Fund, and University of North Carolina Chapel Hill Julius L. Chambers Distinguished Professor of Law

"Anthony Carter offers readers his most intimate and precious thoughts and experiences, his unbreakable faith, and his inspiring optimism. Compassionate, unwaveringly honest, and startlingly modest, he gives you a strong sense of the moral and social justice that defines the amazing and very accomplished man I am privileged to know."

—Kim Bepler, Philanthropist and Fordham University Trustee

"The pages of this book emanate well-practiced joy. In *This I Know,* Anthony Carter has given us a series of powerful vignettes and timely encouragement to inspire sustained and active reflection on how our unique vocational paths can better illuminate God's dream for our world in all its wondrous diversity. Anthony writes with the determined delight of a man who has discovered a pearl of great price and won't rest until it's been shared far and wide. Drawing on years of lived experience as a man of faith, of humility, and of hope, Anthony leverages his business acumen to deliver a series of short, practical lessons in living for and with others. This slender volume carries a weighty message, inviting us to encounter anew a God who embraces all."

—Eric A. Clayton, award-winning author of, among other books, *Cannonball Moments: Telling Your Story, Deepening Your Faith* and *Finding Peace Here and Now: How Ignatian Spirituality Leads Us to Healing and Wholeness*

"Anthony Carter has been a mentor, guide, and inspiration in my journey to lead with authenticity and courage. His example taught me that true leadership is rooted in faith, conviction, and humanity, and that our greatest responsibility is to empower others to do the same. *This I Know* is an invitation to all of us to lean into faith, embrace our convictions, celebrate our differences, and commit ourselves to the greater good of humanity. Anthony shows us how possible, and how fulfilling, it is to embrace our best selves and serve humanity with purpose."

—Smita Pillai, Mom, Wife, Daughter, Friend, Global Citizen, Senior Vice President of Culture, Inclusion & Development, Regeneron Pharmaceuticals

"I have known Anthony Carter for more than thirty years, first as a colleague and later as a friend, and I always sensed he was someone special. In *This I Know,* we discover why: Anthony has walked the long road to faith, optimism, love, and God—and invites us to join him. With honesty and courage, he weaves his own story with the wisdom of Emerson, Dr. King, and Scripture. Whether you are a devout Catholic, like Anthony, or simply seeking encouragement in living a meaningful life, this book will move and inspire you."

—John Doorley, author, thought leader in reputation management and public and corporate communications, also one of the people Anthony Carter mentions who nagged him to write this book

"In a time when negativity dominates so much of our culture, *This I Know* is a refreshing and uplifting reminder of what unites us rather than what divides us. The author's openness in sharing his personal journey, together with his boldness in addressing difficult controversial topics, offers readers nothing less than a master class in how to live with decency, honesty, integrity, kindness, purpose, and faith. Each chapter challenges us to imagine what our world could become if we all embraced these principles in our daily lives. I was deeply touched by this powerful book. I have no doubt the world will be touched as well."

—Ralph D. Weaver, Founding President, East West Connection and Joy Connection, Connector, Caretaker, Loyal Friend, Grandfather, Husband

"*This I Know* is a captivating read. In it, we meet Anthony Carter, whose stories show how we too can live with love, joy, and integrity—and make a difference in the world. Working with Anthony on a global leadership project, I witnessed firsthand how his vision and commitment changed the trajectory of many lives, produced outstanding leaders, and demonstrated the transformative power of a leader whose mind, body, and spirit are aligned with the Creator. **This I know:** Anthony Carter is a messenger for diversity, sent from above."

—Juan T. Lopez, President, Amistad Associates

"Anthony Carter's *This I Know* is a masterpiece on the journey of African Diaspora people through the Catholic Faith. His testimonies ring true to not only the Black Catholic experience but also to the American experience itself. I was affirmed and inspired every time I turned a page."

—Dr. Ansel Augustine, DMin, lay minister and author of *Praying with Our Feet*

"From the earliest stages, I was drawn to Anthony Carter's story—its honesty, courage, and deep faith were impossible to ignore. Seeing *This I Know* come to life has been profoundly rewarding, and I couldn't be happier with how this inspiring book turned out."

—Gary Jansen, Executive Editor, Loyola Press, and award-winning author of, among other books, *Meditations at Midnight*

I was taught to do my best, try my hardest,
and keep striving up the ladder.
But at each rung I was to reach back and help
a brother, sister, or stranger
receive the gift and pass it on, and thus help
create a more caring, sharing world.

—Thea Bowman

*PRINCIPLES FOR A LIFE OF FAITH AND OPTIMISM*

# THIS I KNOW

**ANTHONY P. CARTER**

*FOREWORD BY*

*DENZEL WASHINGTON*

LOYOLA PRESS.
A JESUIT MINISTRY

LOYOLA PRESS.
A JESUIT MINISTRY
www.loyolapress.com



Cover art credit: Katsumi Murouchi/Moment/Getty Images, Olena Malik/Moment/Getty Images
Interior art credit: VladSt/DigitalVision Vectors/Getty Images
Author photo credit: Wendy O. Carter

ISBN: 978-0-8294-6011-7
Library of Congress Control Number: 2025944729

Published in Chicago, IL
Printed in the United States of America
25 26 27 28 29 30 31 32 33 34 Versa 10 9 8 7 6 5 4 3 2 1

This book is dedicated to my wife, Wendy.
When I count my blessings
you are first on the list.

# Contents

# Foreword

## by Denzel Washington

You know who I am and what I do for a living.

The person many of you may not know is my dear friend Anthony Carter. Anthony and I have been friends for fifty-four years and counting. With a bit of self-pride, I can tell you there are few of Doc's friends who know him as well as I do.

I call him Doc—a nickname he earned when we both majored in premed at Fordham University. When you read Anthony's story, you'll understand why I admire him, and why I'm proud to be his friend. He is a loving husband, father, and grandfather. He is also a man of faith. His love of God is powerful and enduring.

This is a book about Doc's impact on so, so many people, and the impact they've had on him. Yes, he's had a stellar career in corporate communications, diversity, public service, and volunteerism. Yes, he's the recipient of global awards and recognition. And yet, he will tell you that awards and accolades don't hold a candle to the love he has for, and receives from, his wife, his grown children, his grandson, and his faith.

As you read *This I Know*, you will encounter Doc's faith. There is no doubt that Doc has been called to serve, and he brings his full authentic self in service to others. He cares because he sees the hands of God in all things. You will be moved by his thoughts, perspectives, and ideas. I was. You will enjoy his testimonials and experiences. I did. And after you read this book, trust me, you too will know and admire my dear friend Doc.

**It took me a long time and much painful boomeranging of my expectations to achieve a realization everyone else appears to have been born with: That I am nobody but myself.**

**When I discover who I am, I'll be free.**

RALPH ELLISON

*INVISIBLE MAN*

# Preface

***This I know:*** I am a fervent believer in the One and Only. I see God at the center of everything. I am a Black Catholic blessed with a spouse sent from heaven. I am a retired chief diversity officer for a global healthcare company. I still believe diversity matters. I ride the New York City Subway not only to get to my destination but also to snatch quick peeks of cultural diversity at its finest. I've met and worked with prominent civil rights and political leaders. I have a best friend who has touched the hearts and souls of millions of people across the globe and most likely touched yours, too. We found each other at a critical time, and I can say with certainty that our friendship has made all the difference in my life. I am a graduate of a Jesuit university in New York and currently a trustee of that university. I am a proud father and grandfather. I am a dreamer. I am a percussionist who plays Latin conga drums and African djembe drums. I am an honest, trustworthy man with a sense of humor. I love to make people laugh, and I love to laugh at myself—because as human beings we can do some embarrassingly silly stuff at times.

***This I know:*** While we are living life one day at a time, going forward one step at a time, we aren't fully aware of either the passage of time or the great distance we're traveling. I wrote this book to share what I know. Because when I look back over my career, even *I* am astounded at my journey. That an orphaned, isolated, heartbroken little kid from the Bronx would go where I have gone, learn what I have learned, and become the person I am is a story that defies all the odds.

And yet, it happened.

***This I know:*** It happened because I walk in faith, and I lead with optimism. What do these two choices look like in real life? Well, walking in faith sometimes means that before I enter a high-powered boardroom where decisions will be made that influence the lives of thousands of people, I find a quiet spot and center myself in prayer. It sometimes means that even when I am confused or disheartened, my faith reassures me that I don't necessarily need to understand; I need only to trust. And this is where the optimism comes in. Trust is another word for faith, and having confidence that doing what is right and honorable will work out in the end means that I can lead with optimism. And so I believe in God, and I believe that God will set things straight. That I have the chance to contribute my own personal efforts to the work at hand is a privilege that I find thrilling.

***This I know:*** I am many things, but at my core I am an optimist who believes in the power of love, the power of solidarity, the power of every one of us to connect and come together to make good things happen. Like you, I am all heart and soul.

***This I know:*** As I travel through the corridor of life, even though I'm retired and my children are grown, I know I have a long way to go. I have more footprints to make. Where will they lead me? Well, that's something I *don't* know. What I *do* know about where I'm going is that Someone is watching over me to help me keep moving in the right direction. In his song "Tell My Feet," musician Vinx put into words my guiding philosophy: *Once there, I'll tell my feet I made it Home.*

These are the basic elements of my story.

But I don't look like my story. No one does.

**It is impossible to tell,**
**from a single glance, the journeys**
**someone has traveled,**
**the experiences that have made**
**them who they are.**

STEVE PEMBERTON

## CHAPTER 1

# No One Looks Like Their Story

I've ridden the New York City Subway more times than I can count. When I was a child, it was a joy ride. As a teenager, it was an adventure. As an adult, it was my mode of transportation to and from work.

The subway offers us one of the most exciting experiences we can have in a day because we come in contact with a marvelously diverse conglomeration of humankind. Traveling on an underground train, we will find dancers, singers, and musicians; the rich, the poor, and the unhoused; the fashionistas, the barely dressed, and the overdressed; wailing babies, high-spirited teenagers, and sleep-deprived grad students. You name it. They're right there sitting beside us and across from us. Just like us, they've gone underground, but only temporarily, because this is how they get where they're going.

The objective of the underground subway is to transport passengers from one location to another in the most direct, speedy way possible. Subways allow people to forego the hassle of hailing taxicabs or riding slow-moving city buses. In 2023, the Metropolitan Transit Authority (MTA) reported that the New York City Subway System accounts for 3.6 million daily riders or 1.15 billion annual paid rides.

One unavoidable, if not irresistible, way to pass time spent underground on the subway is to engage in the art of watching other people without them knowing they're being watched. I call this method of unobtrusive observation the underground mirror test. The underground mirror test is not a game. It's an invasion of privacy but it's performed without being overtly invasive. I have a strong suspicion that, whether intentionally or unintentionally, we've all slipped into this subway side effect.

What is the mirror test? It's when we use the windows of the subway while it races through the dark underground tunnels to give us a mirror-like reflection of our fellow passengers. We can look at whomever we want without them knowing. Through these quick glimpses of people we may see only once in our lives, we try to figure out their life stories.

The process may go something like this.

Our first person of interest in the underground mirror is a young Black man who is carrying an overstuffed backpack. He is reading, or pretending to be reading, the advertising plastered in an endless border above the windows on the train. He's dressed in baggy jeans, an oversized T-shirt, and a pair of Air Jordans. A New York Yankees baseball cap worn backwards is on his head. We clutch our pocketbooks a bit more tightly, we cradle our briefcases on our laps.

Next, we sneak a peek at a frumpily dressed, elderly White woman seated with two bulging shopping bags on either side. Her eyes are closed and her head is bouncing in sync with the movement of the jerky subway. We conclude that she is one of many who are unhoused.

The mirror now offers us a view of a Hispanic man standing next to us. Our gaze flickers over him with a quick up-and-down scan. He's dressed in a tailored dark blue suit, starched white shirt, and perfectly knotted tie, and he's sporting a pair of the shiniest brown, unscuffed Oxford shoes you've ever seen. He is, as they say, dressed to the nines. We decide he must be a lawyer at a large firm in Manhattan.

As the subway continues through the tunnel, our attention shifts to another image in the window. An attractive young woman in a form-fitting, colorful, floral dress who has air buds in her ears is rocking out to music only she can hear. Her face is perfectly made up. Her puckered lips are painted shimmering, bright red. Her hair with its vibrant blonde highlights seems a bit over the top for daytime. She must be working the streets tonight. Sheesh!

So, what do we do with this surreptitiously gathered data? We assess. We make assumptions. And we reach conclusions.

The young Black man with the backpack: Well, he's definitely up to no good. He's most likely waiting until the train stops at the next station so he can grab somebody's purse on the way out the door and sprint away into the crowd. However, we may be surprised to learn that in the stuffed backpack are thick textbooks for the chemistry class he's taking at the college he attends, which is two stops up the line. This man is a premed student.

The apparently houseless woman who is holding tightly to her shopping bags while she dozes has just finished a long shift as a room attendant at the luxurious hotel where she has worked for decades. Her bags are filled with fresh produce and groceries so she can whip up a king's meal to celebrate her husband's seventieth birthday.

The dapper Dan we presumed to be a lawyer, is actually someone who recently lost his job, and today he is dressed for a make-it-or-break-it job interview. His partner, who said, "Hey, put these on for your interview—this is my good luck outfit, and I want you to wear it," opened his closet and shared the best of everything he owns to help his partner get the job.

Oh, yes—and the dolled-up, sexy young woman? She's a model who just left a photo shoot and is running late for the next one. She listens to upbeat playlists so that she brings fresh energy and happy vibes into the next shoot. The subway will get her to her next modeling assignment much faster than a taxi.

The point here is that, in the absence of knowing someone's story, we create invalid, insensitive, and inaccurate assessments based on inconclusive evidence. When we do this, we are always more wrong than we are right. This stems largely from the fact that we all have unconscious biases. These types of biases occur because, not knowing anything about the person we just sized up, it's easy to manufacture what we *want* to believe about a person. Our assumptions are based upon personal data, much of which we cannot prove, that has been stored away in our brains. The fact is, we know someone's story only when it is revealed by the person to whom the story belongs.

Today's subway passengers, straphangers as they are called, still playing the underground mirror game, ride with less trepidation. That is because the subway represents the purest form of multicultural heterogeneity, which makes us more curious than fearful. We see ourselves woven into the fabric of diverse and cultural nuances. We are intrigued rather than disturbed by what we see underground. We normalize our experiences. Our character is formed in the crucible of the subway system even though we put up our safeguards and remain watchful. Amid our foibles and in the most magnanimous ways, we represent the beauty and power of diversity.

Often, our outward appearance doesn't fully reflect the complexities and nuances of our inner lives or the stories they carry. Surface-level judgment allows us to make quick assessments based on appearances while failing to recognize the depth and complexity of others. No one looks like their story, and none of us should try to size up a person we know nothing about. We cannot understand someone's life just by looking at them. In almost every case, we will be wrong.

**This I know:**

Every person embodies a story that deserves compassion, not assumptions.

**Most Black Catholic churchgoers are racial minorities in their congregations, unlike White and Hispanic Catholics and Black Protestants.**

PEW RESEARCH CENTER STUDY

## CHAPTER 2

# The Dichotomy of Being Black and Catholic

I am Black. I am Catholic. And I'm proud of being a Black Catholic.

But being a Black Catholic can be hard.

It's difficult even for someone like me, who spent eighteen years of my life—elementary school, high school, and college—in the Catholic school system. As a youngster, I served as an altar boy back when Mass was celebrated in Latin. (I can still recite a few of the Latin prayers!) Later, I served as a lector and played percussion in the music ministry. Today, I am a second-degree Knights of Columbus, which is a Catholic fraternal service order founded in 1882. And I serve as a trustee at Fordham University, a Catholic Jesuit university in New York City.

There is no question that being Black and Catholic is made more difficult because we're a racial minority in our congregations. There are approximately three million Black Catholics in the United States, according to a report published by the Pew Research Center in 2022. We comprise a small share (6%) of Black adults and an even smaller share (4%) of Catholic adults. We are less likely than White or Hispanic Catholics (who make up the vast majority of Catholics in the U.S.) to worship in parishes where most of the parishioners share either their race or their ethnicity. But these are small things compared to other reasons why it is hard to be Black and Catholic.

Having a strong affiliation to the Catholic Church means that there are times when I must reconcile my belief in God with the atrocities committed against Black Americans. When I was a young boy, I watched Dr. Martin Luther King, Jr. deliver powerful speeches and lead peaceful protests. I witnessed the mass exodus of my White neighbors from my South Bronx neighborhood. I was bussed across town to a predominantly White Catholic high school. My guidance counselor advised me to continue my education in a trade school rather than pursue college. Then, there was the searing experience of attending Mass in the Little Italy section of the Bronx when the priest walked down the aisle and refused to shake my outstretched hand during the offering of peace. A young child, Catholic or not, should never be dismissed by a priest.

Ironically, these experiences did not fill me with hate. They did make me curious though.

My curiosity led me to St. Raymond High School for Boys and then to Fordham University, both in New York. While in high school and college I sank deeply into theology and Catholic culture. I was taught by Christian Brothers at St. Raymond and while at Fordham much of my learning came from the Jesuits.

St. Raymond is located in Parkchester, a Bronx neighborhood that at the time was populated predominantly by White folks. Right across the street was the elementary school. Two blocks away was St. Raymond Academy, our sister school, and just a few blocks from there was St. Raymond Catholic Church. Parkchester was very much a closed community. People with my skin color were a rare commodity and were not warmly accepted in the neighborhood. In 1967, Brother Andrew O'Gara, principal of the boy's high school, reached out to several Catholic elementary schools in the South Bronx to recruit Black and Latino eighth grade students to come to St. Raymond. His intention was to bring in a diverse array of students who would enhance the overall learning experience so that we all would be prepared for college and the real world once we graduated. I entered St. Raymond in 1968. It was my first experience of being in the classroom with predominantly White students. Truthfully, it didn't feel as awkward as I expected because Black and Latino students were welcomed into the school. St. Raymond High School was my first crack at being in a diverse community even before I fully understood what cultural diversity meant. Brother Andrew's courageous plan, or, some would say, experiment, worked.

I graduated from St. Raymond in 1972 and began my next academic journey in that same year at Fordham University on the picturesque Rose Hill Campus in the Bronx, New York. Rose Hill is an eighty-five-acre gated community featuring Gothic architecture and tree-lined walkways. One of the most prized possessions on the campus is an American elm tree that is almost three hundred years old and is a crowned champion in the National Registry of Champion Trees. At that point in my life, experiencing this type of exposure to Mother Nature's environmental splendor was beyond my wildest imagination. Sculptured gardens with the most exotic species of plants and flowers you can imagine grew across the street from Fordham in the Botanical Gardens. And just a ten-minute walk south of the campus was the Bronx Zoo, where childlike adventure came alive every time anyone stepped foot into the animal kingdom.

I studied journalism at Fordham. I wrote for two of the university's newspapers—*The Ram* and *The Paper*—and co-hosted a weekly talk show on the Fordham radio station, WFUV. In each role, I understood that my job was to deliver fair and balanced reporting to students, faculty, and the tri-state listening audience across New York, New Jersey, and Connecticut.

One of my most cherished assignments as a student journalist for *The Ram* was having the opportunity to interview Julian Bond, a leading figure in the early civil rights movement. While he was a student at Morehouse College, Bond was a founding member of the Student Nonviolent Coordinating Committee (SNCC), the principal channel of student commitment in the United States to the civil rights movement during the 1960s. In 1975, the Fordham student government club invited Bond to speak at the Rose Hill campus, where he delivered a speech titled "The Apotheosis of the New Era." It was one of the most profound and insightful talks I'd ever heard about one person's journey in the fight for justice, equality, and fairness. He shared personal stories about his involvement in the civil rights period, including sit-ins at lunch counters, being hosed to the ground while bottles and rocks were thrown at him, and being beaten with batons by police. After his remarks, he and I sat together for ninety minutes discussing his commitment to social justice, and the painful yet glorious era of fighting for the rights of Black Americans.

Ten years later, we met at a convention sponsored by the National Association for the Advancement of Colored People (NAACP), the largest and oldest civil rights organization in America. He remembered our discussion at Fordham and asked if I could send him the article I had written about his visit to the campus. It just so happened I kept that article and was able, and delighted, to send him a copy.

My Catholic education prepared me for life and for my role as chief diversity officer at Johnson & Johnson, where I reported directly to the chairman and CEO. In that position, I learned that once you declare personal accountability and demonstrate strong leadership, you can address issues of diversity and racial injustice in thoughtful and decisive ways. How? Well, one of the principles of Jesuit teaching is to discern, and discernment was a tool that was invaluable to me in my career.

Still, some of my Black friends believe being Black and Catholic is oxymoronic. This is because Black Americans have a troubling history with the Catholic Church. There was a time when Blacks were not allowed to even take part in Catholic rituals like serving at the altar or receiving Communion. Many Blacks still feel the pains of these indignities. Many changed their religious affiliations.

My faith fortifies my belief that God does not categorize his love for us based upon race, color, gender, or sexual orientation. I believe that our differences are our strengths. They are an adhesive that unites us.

I am thrilled that the Catholic Church was blessed by the leadership of our beloved Pope Francis, may he rest in peace. He was a change agent, and during his tenure he started to help mend the indignities many Black Catholics feel. Taking its cue from Pope Francis, the United States Conference of Catholic Bishops (USCCB) formed an anti-racism committee and publicly stated, "Recent events have exposed the extent to which the sin of racism continues to afflict our nation. The establishment of this new ad hoc committee will be wholly dedicated to engaging the Church and our society to work together in unity to challenge the sin of racism, to listen to persons who are suffering under this sin, and to come together in the love of Christ to know one another as brothers and sisters."

While this is a courageous and welcome step forward by the church, there remains more to be done. I encourage church leaders at the local level to explicitly denounce all forms of racism. As a Black Catholic, hearing priests at the pulpit discuss racism with the same strong sense of concern given to people experiencing homelessness, hunger, poverty, and illness would be a meaningful and encouraging sign of solidarity. The Pew Research Center study cited at the beginning of this chapter also found that Black Catholics are more likely than White or Hispanic Catholics to say that opposition to racism and sexism is essential to what being a faithful Christian means to them.

It is important to encourage anti-racism committees similar to the committee formed by the USCCB at the local level as well. We must embolden congregations across the country to engage in discussions on issues like police brutality, and the mass incarceration of Blacks and Brown-skinned people. By highlighting experiences faced by Black Catholics and by celebrating the richness of our culture, parishes can create concrete signs of solidarity and inclusion.

If we are to foster an inclusive Catholic community, one that truly reflects all of God's goodness, then no one should ever feel unwelcome. And maybe, just maybe, more Black folks will show up at church readily able to practice their Catholic faith.

**This I know:**

It is possible to hold deep faith and deep pain at the same time, and yet still believe in a Church that can grow more just and inclusive.

**Are not all angels spirits in the divine service, sent to serve for the sake of those who are to inherit salvation?**

HEBREWS 1:14

## CHAPTER 3

# When Love Knocks, Answer

We live in a world filled with all types of technology gadgets. Take the doorbell for instance. A smart doorbell has a camera that allows you to screen visitors. When someone approaches your door, they push the doorbell and you, who might be somewhere inside the house, or not—maybe you're typing up a report in your office miles away from home—hear the sound of a ringtone chime. You open your smartphone to see the image of a person standing at your front door. You have a choice to make: Respond to the person through your smartphone or ignore the person altogether. When and if you respond, you can create the impression that, assuming you're even home, you're unable to come to the door. You have the advantage of knowing what's going on outside while the guest doesn't have a clue regarding your actual whereabouts.

Forty-one years ago, there was a knock on my door. I was typing a report on an IBM Selectric typewriter in my twenty-first-floor office at 9 West 57th Street, the corporate headquarters of Avon Products, Inc., a forty-nine-story tower and one of the most prominent, distinctive buildings in New York City. Through the large window overlooking the picturesque gold coast of New York City's Central Park, I could see brilliant sunshine spilling out upon velvety green grass. The full cast of tree characters—the tall oaks, the elms, the cherry, and the maples—were standing at attention in all their resplendent glory. The view was so special, sometimes colleagues would come into my office just to sneak a peek at the gold coast. I had positioned my typewriter so that every time I typed I could escape into that view with just a glance. Gazing at that magnificence gave me creative energy while I worked.

I turned around to see who was knocking on my door. I almost fell out of my chair. To my amazement, there stood a very beautiful woman. She was impeccably and stylishly dressed, and on her glowing, mocha-colored face was a smile that lit up the room. I mustered enough cool to stand up as I always do when someone enters my office, and I greeted this unexpected guest with a cordial good morning. "Hi!" she said. "I'm here to meet you." Something inside me exclaimed, *Wow! There* is *a God!* She continued. "My name is Wendy Olga Willoughby." How crazily coincidental. Her initials—WOW—captured my initial reaction. *Wow!*

I invited Wendy into my office, and we talked for a while. She told me that many of her friends who were mutual acquaintances asked if she knew me since we worked at the same company. When she told them she did not, they urged her to reach out.

What would have happened if I had not answered the knock on the door?

My backstory at this point in my life was that I had been married for ten years. The first five were fine. The last five were tumultuous and lacking in joy and happiness. On the exterior, I pretended all was good. Inside, I was broken—the results of an unhealthy marriage. We ultimately determined the marriage we had was not the best thing for us.

The reality was that God was not present in the marriage. I had allowed my faith to be crushed by living with a partner whose faith did not align with mine.

So, we divorced.

At first, the failed marriage embarrassed me, but over time I came to understand that it was the right thing to do. The best thing about that marriage is that we gave birth to two beautiful children, Austin and Ashley. In fact, in addition to immersing myself in my work, what had kept me sane during the five years since we had divorced was the joy I found in co-parenting Austin and Ashley. Nurturing my children helped me manage the pain. My kids were my lifeline, and they helped me find peace again. I had no interest in remarrying or even dating; I simply loved being a dad.

Wendy became a close friend. I never expected more than that. I shared stories with her. Good ones. Bad ones. Funny ones. Sad ones. She did not judge. She just listened. In being that kind of friend, she allowed me to become better at listening and being nonjudgmental. I began to laugh again. I found solace in someone else's company, even though we were not, as they say, "an item." Unlike me, however, Wendy was dating.

The miracle of Wendy is that she helped restore my faith in God. I was broken and I felt isolated. I was afraid to ask God for help because I believed I had done something wrong in divorcing my wife. Not seeing my children every day had been, for me, unimaginable. How would that impact my role as a father? How would they know I still loved them if I was not a daily presence in their lives? Not living in the same home with my children was difficult to understand and accept. Having visitations and joint custody—talk about *hurt*.

Thank God, having Wendy in my life helped ease the pain of being apart from my children.

Wendy is a devoted Catholic and her faith runs deep. We began seeing more of each other. Our friendship turned into romance. I proposed, she said yes. Thirty-six years later, here we are, stronger and more in love than ever. Thirty-two years ago, we brought a new Carter into the world, our son Dayne. Wendy, Austin, Ashley, and Dayne composed the center of my existence. They formed the structure of my newly found happy place. I felt like me again—*vibrant* and *free*. I belonged to a family that loves me unconditionally.

That unexpected knock by a woman with the initials WOW recharged my life. I believe the knock was an awakening to wholesomeness again. It made my initial reaction—*Wow! There* is *a God!*—more meaningful. At that most vulnerable time in my life, I found my earthly savior, Wendy, who brought me back to God. I *know* she was sent by an angel. Pure in heart, overflowing in kindness, Wendy is the miracle in the doorway who built me back better.

I wrote a poem to Wendy for our first anniversary; it hangs, framed, on the wall in our bedroom.

*Met an angel who invited me into heaven.*
*Doesn't even wear a halo.*
*Stepped into paradise; erased a past clouded with gloom.*
*Has no magic wand.*
*Learned to smile away past nightmares.*
*She brings an abundance of laughter.*
*Soothed by the touch of an innocent spirit,*
*Merely a human soul.*
*Guarded from pain by the presence of a savior.*
*She just holds my hand.*
*Met an angel who offered me a chance at heaven,*
*She takes her wings, and we fly there.*

When life gives you lemons, make lemonade. Or as our son Dayne, who is a basketball enthusiast, would say, "A shot never taken is a shot missed!"

Even if you're still waiting for your angel, you can be an angel.

Knock, knock. Answer the door.

"Wow! There *is* a God!"

**This I know:**

God sometimes shows up disguised as a knock on your door—and healing begins when you're brave enough to answer.

**Whoever walks with the**

**wise becomes wise,**

**but the companion of fools**

**suffers harm.**

PROVERBS 13:20

## CHAPTER 4

# The Price of Friendship

Many years ago, I learned a very important lesson from the mother of a very important person. She told me, "Your friend admires you so much. He told me so. He admires that you have an important job with a big company. You go to work every day. You earn an annual salary. He on the other hand doesn't know when his next job is coming." I replied, "Please excuse me for interrupting, but when my friend takes on just one job, he'll make more money than I can count." We both laughed. "Yes," she answered. "Maybe. But you can't put a price on friendship." I was moved. And she was right: True friendship cannot be monetized.

The mother of this very important person was the late Mrs. Lennis Washington, who passed away on June 14, 2021. She was ninety-seven years old. She was a successful entrepreneur, a woman of principle and faith, and a wonderful mother. She invited me to call her by her first name. I told her I could not do that because I had been raised to address adults properly. She insisted but I resisted. I asked if calling her *Mom* would work. She smiled and said yes.

Her son is Denzel Washington, with whom I've had the joy of sharing fifty-four years of unbroken friendship. Almost every time we talk, he calls attention to the number of years we've been friends and reminds me that many of our other friends are no longer alive.

I already knew how much Denzel meant to me, but Mrs. Washington helped me understand how much I meant to Denzel. If it weren't for her, I might never have realized that my respect for Denzel was reciprocated.

He and I share a brotherhood different from what I had with my siblings growing up. My mother died when I was six and my father when I was seven, leaving ten children: five boys and five girls spanning infancy to twenty years old. Except for our oldest sister and two oldest brothers, we were separated and cared for by aunts, uncles, godparents, and close neighbors. I was taken in by my godmother, who had an apartment in the same five-story tenement building where my family lived when my parents were alive.

Sadly, I grew up having only vague memories of a childhood with my brothers and sisters. The sting was not knowing my family, especially my brothers. Once I attended a New York Knicks basketball game at Madison Square Garden with friends. I noticed my brother sitting by himself in a nearby section. We glanced at each other. All we could do was nod and wave. Yet I couldn't stop staring across the rows, *watching* my brother watching the game.

My mother's presence in the neighborhood was sorely missed. Neighbors would tell me stories about how calm and caring she was to everyone. I remember when I was four years old and sitting on my mother's lap crying while my sisters and brothers headed out the door for school each morning. I cried because I wanted so badly to go to school too, but I wasn't old enough. I will never forget sitting on her lap while she taught me the alphabet and how to print and write cursive style. When I entered first grade, I already knew my ABC's and could write quite well for a little boy.

My father was the disciplinarian. He was certainly not one to spare the rod. He worked as a construction foreman on crews that built tall apartment buildings around New York City. One day, one of the workers who operated the mobile crane on the site of a big project came to work intoxicated and wiped out several workers. My father never came home from work that day. He was one of the casualties of that disaster.

My godmother, who raised me from that time on, was a proud woman. She worked as an emergency room nurse in a hospital in the South Bronx. She raised me during turbulent times when fires, gangs, and drugs were rampant. She was strict. Very strict. She would always tell me her job was to keep me on the straight and narrow so that I could grow up and become somebody. Her favorite saying was *It's easy to get into trouble, but it's hard to get out.* She had high but simple goals for me: She wanted me to graduate from college, be a good human being, and be a loving husband and father. Oh yeah . . . and becoming a doctor would have been the icing on her cake. But the tragedy is that she was the meanest person I ever knew.

She kept me in a constant state of fear using physical violence so extreme, it affected the whole neighborhood. After the beatings, I saw sympathy and pain in the eyes of our neighbors, felt tenderness in their hugs.

I remember watching with sadness as my neighborhood playmates scampered home at dinnertime, while my feet dragged as I trudged slowly to my godmother's apartment. A small voice within kept reminding me to be thankful because having somewhere to go kept me safe from the gangs that roamed the streets. I just wished I could go home to any other place than *that* one.

My heart was always heavy with longing. I longed for home. For family. For a feeling of belonging and a sense of identity. Most of all, I longed for my mother. I longed for her love. Not a day went by that I didn't wish she was alive.

In many ways, Denzel is a gift from God. He is the brother I yearned for to fill the emptiness and heartbreak I had experienced as an orphaned child. I didn't have a brother physically present when I needed one most. Someone who would share the joys and struggles and pains of life.

One of Denzel's strongest, most admirable attributes is his love of God; another is his humility. During the many years we've known each other, we've never had any interruption in our friendship. Never an argument. Never a fight. Never a misunderstanding. I give him all the credit. He is an exceptional human being.

I've shared moments with Denzel while he was in character, listening to him rehearse his lines for a movie or Broadway production. I remember Denzel reciting sections from one of his scripts, speaking to me as if I were one of the characters on the set. Utterly amazed, I asked him how in the world he remembers all this stuff. He smiled. With that intense "Denzel stare," he explained, "I allow God to work through me. I am his instrument."

Denzel and I met in 1972 on the Rose Hill campus of Fordham University during our freshman year. Both of us were enrolled in the premed program; both of us hoped to become doctors one day. We would stroll side by side through the eighty-plus acres of Fordham's picturesque Bronx campus, heading to our biology class with childlike enthusiasm, imagining becoming doctors while simultaneously wondering if we had chosen the right field of study. Maybe we had. At least for the most part we were excited about the possibilities.

In the biology lab, we experimented on all kinds of interesting things, like dissecting a Drosophila melanogaster (fruit fly) in order to analyze its minuscule anatomy. On another day, we would prick our finger with a sterilized needle, take a drop of blood, and examine it on a slide beneath the microscope, wondering *What on earth are we looking for*? But the real problem was that it took nearly the entire two-hour lab session to muster up the courage to push the needle into my finger. And when I did, I had to turn away because I couldn't stomach the sight of a minute drop of blood popping out of my finger. Embarrassing? Yes.

Denzel and I laughed about this. Eventually, though, we realized we were experimenting in a field of study where the results were not going to be favorable for either one of us.

Our grades in biology were not pretty. (They were abysmal.) Reality kicked in, and it kicked hard. Midway through the first semester, we asked ourselves, Do we stay in premed and flunk out? Or do we find something else that we would really love to do? Together, we talked it through. We decided that premed was not where we wanted to be—or should be—and we thought about how we would tell our families about our decision to abandon the program. In my case, my godmother would have been devastated if she knew that I was switching majors. I didn't even tell her until I graduated. She was shocked; I was liberated.

But Denzel told his mother immediately. He let her know he was dropping premed to pursue theater. Her response was humorous yet direct: "Well, son, you've always been an actor. No surprise. Go for it! You'll be good at it." With that reaction, Mrs. Washington showed me what optimism and unconditional love looked like in real life.

We withdrew from the premed program and switched to communications, with Denzel studying theater while I studied journalism. Good call for us both. Our grades began to move in the right direction. We never looked back. And the rest is history. (By the way, one of Denzel's earliest roles as an actor was in the television series *St. Elsewhere*, in which he was cast as a medical doctor, Dr. Philip Chandler. How coincidental! He became a doctor after all, something we laugh about even today.)

In our sophomore year as communications students, we lived on campus in the same suite in the Martyrs' Court dormitory. We maintained our ritual of walking to class together, studying together, and doing our assignments side by side. Denzel was from Mount Vernon, New York, about thirty minutes from campus. I was from the South Bronx, which is about a twenty-minute bus ride away. With home so close to the university, it would have been easy to commute, but we chose to live on campus because remaining in our neighborhoods while attending college would not have been the right call. We loved our communities. We built strong friendships with many who are still in our lives today. But because of the unhealthy distractions that existed—distractions such as gang warfare and drugs—it was better to live in a place where we could focus on our studies. And that safe haven was Fordham.

What were the odds of becoming friends with one of the biggest movie stars in the world? Who would have thought he'd be the best man in my wedding, and I a groomsman in his? Or that Denzel would be my daughter's godfather, and I the godfather of his oldest son?

How could this be? Or better yet, *why* did this happen?

It's called *maktub*, an Arabic word which roughly means *it is written* or *destiny*. In popular religion it might be called fate or something that is predetermined. I didn't go to college to become friends with one of the world's most recognized people. At that point in our lives, Denzel and I were mostly concerned with whether we were going to flunk out! As fate would have it, we did just fine. In fact, we did very well—well enough to be the recipients of honorary doctorates from our alma mater.

I often ask myself what would have happened if we hadn't met. I don't know. What I do know is that this is a cherished friendship, and one of the most important relationships in my life.

Always aware of and grateful for our blessings, what is of utmost importance to Denzel and me is our love of God and our love of family; these aspects of our lives are nonnegotiable. We were both also taught to treat everyone with respect and kindness. Upon these values our friendship was built.

Late one evening Denzel and I, along with our wives Pauletta and Wendy, were strolling the streets of New York City after enjoying a wonderful dinner together. As we were taking in the sights of the tall buildings and the hustle and bustle of the crowds, two young men in their late teens or early twenties—with hoodies covering their heads and concealing their faces and with their hands in their pockets—came running from the other side of the avenue toward Denzel. As I watched the scene unfold, I sensed danger and went into action. I jumped in between the two youngsters and Denzel, and in a loud voice asked, "What's up?" They removed their hands from their pockets, pulled back their hoodies, and with beaming smiles asked me if they could get Mr. Washington's autograph. Without missing a beat, Denzel walked towards the young men and said, "Of course!" They took out their magic markers and asked if he would sign their hoodies. He did.

When all was done, Wendy pulled me by the arm with a look on her face that could frighten an army of soldiers and said, "What in the world were you thinking by jumping in the middle of that? You could have been hurt!"

"I was protecting Denzel."

"You're not his bodyguard, you're his friend!"

We all laughed. She was right. However, I thought my friend was going to be attacked, and what do friends do for their friends? They look out for each other.

Some years ago, I was sitting with a bunch of friends who knew that Denzel and I are close. One person asked if I thought he was a great actor. I paused. I didn't have an immediate answer. It was a tough question. I thought a bit and told them that because our relationship runs deeper, I see Denzel as more than that. I see him first as a man of principle, someone who is determined, focused, and disciplined. I know him to be a generous, unselfish human being. He is a great husband, a great father, and a great friend who is incredible at whatever he does.

But to answer the question, yes, he is a great actor. I've seen just about every movie and theatre production he's been in. I've been on the sets of many of his movies and I've watched rehearsals for a few of his Broadway productions. Not too long ago I saw him in the first-ever Broadway production of *Othello*, and he was fantastic. I've stayed up late to watch his appearances on the late-night talk shows.

But it's the fifty-four years of solid friendship that humble me and make me feel so very lucky.

Denzel tells a story about a woman in his mother's beauty parlor who stared at him through the mirror and then wrote something on a piece of paper. As she was leaving the salon, she handed him a note which said, *You're going to travel the world and preach to millions of people.* What a powerful prediction! Denzel has accomplished what this prophetess had prophesied.

What amazes me about Denzel's achievements is that he is still the same utterly grounded, unfailingly humble man he was when we first met. But more than anything, it is his faith that allows me to appreciate his greatness, because Denzel's devotion to God is unrivaled. Denzel often reminds me that man gives the award, but God gives the reward.

Denzel and I have done well in our careers, yet we see our friendship as one of the most important achievements of our lives. What we have been blessed with is rare, and there's no way anyone could put a price on it.

Do you have a Denzel in your life? Someone who is true, and staunch, and with you all the way?

What do you do for others that gives you a purpose-driven life? Is it mentorship? Is it being a proud brother or a nurturing sister? Is it being a loving, supportive spouse, parent, grandparent, auntie, or uncle? Do you get goose bumps when someone tells you that you mean the world to them?

Whatever the relationship might be, is it guided by faith?

I've heard Denzel allude to Proverbs 13 often: *Walk with the wise and become wise.* This verse is a simple reminder that we are the product of the people we surround ourselves with. If we want to grow personally and spiritually, we need to nurture friendships with people who cherish similar goals. And how do I know this? Because the greatest gifts in my life are the people God put into my life. The value of friendship . . . the treasure of a dear friend . . . these gifts are immeasurable.

**This I know:**

A true friend—someone who walks with you through struggle and failure, transformation and joy—is a priceless treasure. Cultivate a true friendship.

**The question is not what you look at,**

**but what you see.**

HENRY DAVID THOREAU

## CHAPTER 5

# Angel 555

It's safe to say that most people have experienced some aspect in their lives in which they have been haunted by something or someone. Haunting isn't necessarily an evil thing. Having something eerie, or eerily meaningful, can be a beautiful thing. Either way, it invites you to pay attention because its presence just might be pertinent to what's going on in your life.

In my senior year at Fordham University, I lived in a dormitory called 555. The dorm was given that name based on its address. It was a twelve-floor, high-rise building that was slightly off—but also technically on—campus. At the time, the building represented an experiment in innovative apartment living for students. Each apartment was composed of a suite consisting of three bedrooms, a kitchen, a bathroom, and a gathering room. I lived on the eleventh floor in Suite 1106. I was a dormitory resident advisor, with responsibility for four floors.

Eerily, as I am writing this sentence, I look up and my iPhone reads 5:55 p.m. Hmm. These three numbers—555—appear to me so often, it's scary. I wake up from a deep sleep, and the digital clock on my night table reads 5:55 a.m. I sit in the kitchen talking with my wife, and I happen to glance at the clocks on the microwave and stove. They both read 5:55 p.m. I leave a gas station after filling up my SUV. I drive a few miles. For no reason whatsoever, I look at the gas gauge. It reads 555 miles till empty. When the country experienced a recent spike in gas prices, I drove past one fueling station where a glaring electronic sign was flashing premium gas for $5.55. I see the numbers 555 at the most random times. And yet, I'm not a clock watcher. I don't sit and wait for the numbers to appear. I don't set an alarm for that time. It seems to just . . . *happen.* It feels as if 555 is haunting me. When it finds me, it beckons me to notice its presence. So, I embrace it. After so many appearances, this recurrence must be about more than just numbers. I wonder: In this weird moment in time, is something or someone trying to send me a message?

According to Kyle Gray, author of *Angel Numbers: The Message and Meaning Behind 11:11 and Other Number Sequences*, the numbers 555 are angel messages and calls to action. He urges his readers to open our hearts, arms, and minds to receive the blessings that are offered to us with these messages. For example, if we are working on a project and see 555, it's a sign from heaven to expect success. Kitty O'Callaghan, another author who has written about the meaning of spiritual numbers, says when we see 555 it means the universe is moving things around for us and changes are coming our way. We should prepare for the shifts and waves that are about to roll in. Things are going to get exciting. Thus, a reasonable interpretation of the frequent appearance of these numbers is that angels are urging me to embrace the changes happening in my life, and to trust in the universe's plan for my growth and evolution. I see components of spiritual awakening, trust, faith, manifestation, and abundance in this number.

Before moving to Florida six years ago, Wendy and I lived in New Jersey for seventeen years. We were parishioners at Saint Joseph Parish. On Sunday mornings before and after Mass, our pastor, Father Hank Hilton, greeted parishioners. One particular Sunday our youngest son, Dayne, attended Mass with us. After Mass, we stopped to chat with Father Hank. I introduced him to our son and asked if he would bestow a blessing upon him as he was heading back to college for his sophomore year later that afternoon. Before blessing him, Father Hank asked Dayne what college he attends. "Fordham University," he proudly replied. Father Hank smiled, beamed with joy, and told us that he had graduated from Fordham. "You're kidding!" I said, and then I let him know I graduated from Fordham too. Father Hank asked me what year I graduated. I told him 1976. He graduated two years after I did.

This little chitchat with the pastor got deeper: Not only were we both Fordham graduates but we discovered we also had lived in the same building, 555, and had served as dormitory resident advisors while living in the same Suite 1106. And yet, we didn't come into one another's lives until forty-eight years later. We concluded this discussion so full of surprises with Father Hank bestowing a blessing on Wendy and me, and a special blessing for our son.

What a moment! An unplanned Fordham University reunion!

As a Jesuit, discernment is a big thing in the life of Father Hank. During Mass, he is known for asking his parishioners to pray the following prayer:

*Lord God, help me to know what you want,*
*to want what you want,*
*and to do what you want.*
*Amen.*

For me, praying this prayer offers me an opportunity to discern, to discover ways in which I can understand and make sense of what's going on in our world. In our country. In our behaviors. And in our hearts. And discern what is my accountability for speaking up and speaking out against our inhumanity toward others. How can I better respond to the cries of those who are in need? What is the power given to me by the tenacious hovering of Angel 555?

During the past two years, I have been in conversations with neighbors and friends about the political environment within the United States and around the world. At times, these discussions are intense. However, I have learned that the best I can offer to the dialogue is to just listen. Instead of bickering back and forth, we need to hear one another. When we pray, don't we want God to hear us?

I shared with Denzel the story of Angel 555 and the continuing impact it has on me. He was fascinated. While I was filling him in, he went into high gear doing research on his computer. In no time, he began spouting new information about Angel 555. He brought it all to a head by saying, "I think there's a message here my friend. It's calling you to do something. What do you think it's telling you?"

"One of the things it's telling me is to finish my book."

"Then get busy."

We tend to ignore simple occurrences in our lives. Instead of embracing them, we shrug them off, either because we are frightened by them or because we do not understand them. What if we paid attention to these subtle messages? What if they are messages of enlightenment designed to lead us to a brighter path? What if something in our lives needs to be improved? Especially during times like these when there is so much upheaval and uncertainty in the world, do we heed the messages that might be trying to break through to our awareness? It is possible that they are not as subtle as we would like to believe.

The number 555 beckons me to pay attention, meditate, reflect, trust, act—and share my story. It also makes me wonder, What is haunting *you*? What is prodding *you* to do something that may change your course in life for the better? Could a numerical coincidence, just a series of random numbers, be trying to catch your attention? Could those numbers, like Angel 555, be biblical? Could your message be packed in the occurrence of a certain figure you see in your dreams? Or is it the whisper of the Holy Spirit asking you to collaborate on something new, something beautiful, and important, and redemptive?

We start by paying attention. When we are attentive, we will, as St. Ignatius of Loyola famously observed, see God in everything. There is no doubt that the hand of God is in everything and everyone, and so we should be alert. We should listen. Listen hard for that still, small voice of God. Maybe, just maybe, God is reaching out to us even more than we're reaching out to Him.

These days, this is how I handle the numbers that won't let me go: Every time I see 555, I ask God to tell me what it is He wants me to do. I wait patiently for His response because I know there will be one.

**This I know:**

If you keep seeing the same sign, maybe it's time to stop and listen, because the divine often speaks in repetition.

**Contemplate the diversity**

**of your traditions as a wealth,**

**a wealth willed by God.**

POPE FRANCIS

## CHAPTER 6

# Diversity Is the Heart and Soul of Our Existence

In June of 2024, I had the honor of traveling to Rome on a retreat with the president of Fordham University, Tania Tetlow, and with several of my colleagues who serve as trustees at Fordham, including Board Chair Armando Nuñez, Jr., and members of President Tetlow's leadership team. Two of the objectives for visiting the Holy City were, first, to understand our alignment to the Jesuit mission and identity, and second, to deepen our commitment to the broader Fordham community as trustees. For me, the most pivotal experience was being in the presence of Pope Francis, who had been consistently unwavering in his passion for, commitment to, and appreciation of diversity. His philosophy was beautifully summarized when the pontiff addressed a gathering of young adults attending the Mediterranean Encounters 2024 conference in Tirana, Albania. Pope Francis said, "Unity is not uniformity, and the diversity of our cultural and religious identities is a gift from God."

Diversity is a fact of the human condition. It's how we were made, quite deliberately, by our Creator. Preconceived notions limit us from seeing and experiencing the innate beauty of diversity. My faith tells me that God delights in the differences His human creatures possess.

Before I retired in 2015, I spent the last eight years of my forty-year career managing diversity in corporate America for Johnson & Johnson, ranked forty-second on the 2024 Fortune 500 list of the largest corporations in the United States. Ironically, I'm not as comfortable talking about the topic now as I was then—when I earned a salary for discussing this very thing—especially since there are efforts now to eliminate all aspects of diversity. So instead of looking at what's wrong with diversity, let's talk about what's right about it. First, let me offer some historical and personal context.

The emergence of diversity in the workplace dates back to 1960, when legislation was enacted to prohibit discrimination. In 1961, President John F. Kennedy signed Executive Order 10925, mandating that employees be treated fairly with regard to their race, creed, color, and national origin. This action held companies accountable for diversity under the guidelines of affirmative action and equal employment opportunity. During the 1980s, corporations began to embrace diversity as a management strategy in order to increase the number of women at senior-level positions in the workforce. And in the 1990s and early 2000s, diversity—which, by the way, was not government mandated—was implemented to ensure that all employees were afforded the same opportunities as White men.

From a business perspective, diversity is a management tool that enables companies to enhance their competitive advantage in the marketplace by utilizing an array of exceptional talent from all cultural, educational, geographic, religious, gender, sexual orientation, and racial backgrounds. It is in fact a business advantage.

Prior to my role as chief diversity officer for Johnson & Johnson, I served as vice president of corporate communications. My team and I were responsible for managing internal and external communications for all the corporate functions: human resources, finance, legal, corporate contributions, procurement, government affairs, and the office of diversity. Our responsibilities included preparing speeches for senior executives, putting together global town-hall meetings for employees, media relations, financial reporting, employee communications, and video production.

One day, out of the clear blue, I received a call from Bill Weldon, chairman and CEO of Johnson & Johnson. He asked me to come to his office to talk about the company's progress in diversity. Since the office of diversity was a business partner of mine, it made sense to have this conversation. I was delighted to have an opportunity to talk with Bill about diversity. He knew that it was my passion, as it was his, and I was prepared to have a rich and honest discussion. The meeting began with him wanting to know how, by focusing on diversity as a business imperative, Johnson & Johnson could create an even stronger presence in the workplace and marketplace. We talked about the value of finding solutions to pressing global medical issues like healthcare disparities and unmet medical needs in communities at risk. Diversity was certainly in line with the company's mission of caring for the world one person at a time. It was also in step with the company's credo, which outlines its responsibility to the communities in which we live, work, and serve. We both believed that Johnson & Johnson should be front and center wherever there is a need to extend and enhance life for every human being.

The conversation took an unexpected turn. Looking directly into my eyes, Bill said he wanted me to consider taking on the role of chief diversity officer. Silence. After a gulp (mine) and a few blinks (also mine), I offered Bill what I thought was an appropriate reply: I'm the product of diversity—and, by the way, I'm vice president of corporate communications. I know people I can recommend for this position. This was not the response Bill was expecting. Obviously unimpressed by my answer, he said, "Anthony, I'm the chairman of the board; I know people, too. I'm asking *you* because I want a leader in this role, someone I trust can do the job and get results, and you're that person." Another pause, another gulp. At last, I said, "Whatever you need me to do and believe I can do, I'm in."

I pushed all my chips into the center of the table, so to speak, and worked as hard as I could to help position Johnson & Johnson as a preeminent company in diversity. Indeed, I felt prepared to become the third chief diversity officer in the history of the company, a member of the corporate operating committee, and a C-suite executive, reporting directly to the chairman of the board. I was taking the biggest leap in my career, and I knew it was an important, if not intimidating, opportunity. Having responsibility for this new role, which is to say being responsible for providing the leadership necessary to get this work done, was not lost on me. And I was not about to screw this up.

I learned early in my role that I was more than a diversity practitioner. I was a business partner. What did that mean? First, I had to be knowledgeable about the business imperatives of the various companies within Johnson & Johnson. Second, I had to understand how each business operated so that my team and I could align diversity strategies into each company's business goals and objectives. Third, collectively we had to find ways Johnson & Johnson could leverage its competitive advantage and win in the marketplace with diversity as our strength. We were able to do just that. And Johnson & Johnson was recognized with several diversity awards for the company's leadership performance.

After my first year at this position, and with the staunch support of my team and our colleagues across the enterprise, Johnson & Johnson received an important accolade in the field of diversity: We were recognized by DiversityInc as the number one company for diversity among the top fifty companies in the United States.

DiversityInc—now Fair360—was founded in 1997 as a for-profit company focusing on promoting diversity in the corporate workplace. Each year it organizes an annual awards dinner to publicly recognize the leading companies for their work in diversity. Our objective was not to win awards, and yet it was inspiring to see how our global workforce was energized by this recognition. As a result, Johnson & Johnson appeared on several prominent lists that tracked the best companies for diversity. Our work was highlighted in *Fortune*, *Forbes*, *Savoy*, *Black Enterprise,* and many other magazines and news publications that monitored diversity progress in companies. Members of our diversity staff were invited to speak at conferences and seminars and share case studies. Johnson & Johnson was listed as a company of choice in attracting talented professionals.

We were humbled by the recognition but understood there was lots more hard work ahead. Our work was critical in enhancing the reputation of Johnson & Johnson. I often reflect upon the conversation I had with Bill about taking on the role of chief diversity officer. Back then, I was unable to see what the company could become if we all worked together with aligned goals and objectives. When I retired in 2015, after serving my last eight years in the diversity role, the company gave me a retirement party at corporate headquarters with more than three hundred colleagues in attendance, including my family. The celebration reaffirmed for me that I had put my heart, soul, and mind into the work. I retired from Johnson & Johnson with gratitude and the joy of giving my very best to a company I felt was on the right track with diversity.

Many scholars and practitioners have focused a huge amount of energy on incorporating diversity as a legitimate business practice within corporations across America. One of those scholars, the late Dr. Roosevelt Thomas, Jr., arguably the founding father of strategic diversity management and author of several seminal books on this topic, was my mentor. Dr. Thomas defined diversity as a collective mixture characterized by differences, similarities, and related tensions and complexities. When, back in the day (which is to say when diversity was just called diversity), I served as the chief diversity officer, I was privileged to meet several times with Dr. Thomas, and I recall him saying repeatedly, "Anthony, to get diversity right you must have conceptual clarity." Indeed, he was right. And clarity in applying diversity strategy is more important now than it has ever been.

According to Dr. Thomas, diversity has four components: managing diverse talent, managing relationships, managing representation, and managing all strategic mixtures. Inclusive and diverse cultures propel us into cognitive action in ways that homogeneity does not, all while providing companies with a competitive advantage. In short, diverse teams are better positioned to unlock innovation and drive market growth.

James E. Preston, former chief executive officer of Avon Products, Inc., made it clear when he wrote the foreword to Dr. Thomas's 1991 book *Beyond Race and Gender* that diversity's time had come. Mr. Preston underscored the point that more and more corporations and organizations of all kinds were awakening to the fact that a diverse workforce is not a burden, but the source of their greatest potential strength.

Today, it's unfortunate yet conceivable that those who oppose diversity under the nomenclature of diversity, equity, and inclusion (DEI) feel excluded rather than included when the topic surfaces. Some misunderstand the term *equity*, inferring that only certain groups receive a fair share. And the use of the word *belonging*, which is the most recent addition to the nomenclature, can imply that only certain types of people *belong*. However, diversity as a stand-alone and in its purest sense accommodates everyone. Diversity expunges the feeling of being excluded. It is an essential ingredient when creating a level playing field for everyone—so essential, it was at the center of *everything* we did at Johnson & Johnson. The mission of Johnson & Johnson, then and now, is to extend and enhance human life while caring for the world one person at a time. Unsurprisingly, then, diversity is the heart and soul of the company's existence.

Diversity is more than monitoring a company's head count; it's about saving lives as well. For example, our work in diversity at Johnson & Johnson created opportunities to change the state of healthcare in elementary schools in five cities in the United States. In partnership with a senior technology executive at Microsoft, Michael D. Robinson, and an external team of consultants, the office of diversity converted a collateral-based physical fitness program to a virtual exercise and learning platform called Gateway to a

Healthy Community. The program was designed to keep students moving as they were exploring various aspects of the school's curricula, including geography, history, and culture. In geography, students climb Mount Kilimanjaro while viewing video modules and graphics. This activity, and many other enhancements to the core curricula, resulted in dramatic increases in student acuity, attentiveness, enthusiasm for learning, and higher grades. Among many of the students, there was an increase in healthy eating, resulting in noticeable weight loss.

In the area of health literacy, the office of diversity partnered with Johnson & Johnson medical device businesses to create literature to inform Black and Hispanic men fifty-five years and older of the importance of joint replacement surgery. Studies have documented that the quality of life is significantly enhanced for people in this at-risk population when they get a hip or knee replacement because of arthritis or other related issues. We also developed literature to inform women thirty-three years and older and living in Louisiana about the risk of diabetes.

As a Black Catholic, I agree that the creation of diversity was not simply God's *plan*; it was also His *gift* to humankind. To deny the gift of diversity is as irrational as believing that God will judge us by the color of our skin, or our intellectual capability, or whom we choose to love. It's unthinkable. A world without diversity would be synonymous with listening to a symphony orchestra in which all the instruments were clarinets. It is clear that we are called by God to delight in our differences. Our differences are to be celebrated, appreciated, and exploited for their full range of possibilities, for we all come with different talents, abilities, strengths, and gifts. As a former business leader, and still today a practitioner in this field, I know diversity is at the heart and soul of our identity as well as our existence.

**This I know:**

Diversity isn't a challenge to overcome—it's the very design of God, and a strength that makes us more whole.

**I think that if I was not**

**a man of faith,**

**I'd be scared to death.**

ANDREW YOUNG

---

## CHAPTER 7

# Ironclad Faith

In the fall of 2014, I had the good fortune of spending time with Andrew Young, the former U.S. ambassador to the United Nations appointed by President Jimmy Carter. Ambassador Young also served as the fifty-fifth mayor of Atlanta, Georgia, and as a U.S. congressman. He began his career as a pastor, and he was an early leader in the civil rights movement, becoming a close confidant of Dr. Martin Luther King, Jr. As the executive director of the Southern Christian Leadership Conference, he is credited with being one of the chief architects of both the civil rights and the social justice movements in America.

During one of our meetings, I asked Mr. Young how he was able to respond in a nonviolent way to racists who spit on him, trained the full force of fire hoses upon him, beat him with police batons, and directed vicious dogs to attack and maul him. I'll never forget his response. His face became somber. His eyes widened. He stared at me for a moment that seemed to last forever. He put his fist under his chin and pondered his words. At last he said, "One who practices nonviolence has deep faith that justice will win."

Whoa! I swear I didn't see that coming! I was expecting something quite different from this learned, experienced man—something quite different than his beautifully profound, exquisitely simple, reduced-to-a-nutshell explanation. How could this man, how could Dr. King, how could anyone just stand there and be brutally tortured while singing "We Shall Overcome"? And then align all of this brutish abuse with their faith? In an interview with CNN, Andrew Young said Dr. King once suggested to him that they must both be clinically insane if they think they could change the world. Mr. Young responded to Dr. King by singing a line from one of the old Negro spirituals, "I don't feel no ways tired."

It's hard to make sense of this. This equanimity. This poise. This unflappable response to the world. This Jesus-like point of view. And yet it happened. It happened because it made sense to Mr. Young. It happened because it made sense to Dr. King. And it made sense to the people who rallied around them. Mr. Young's words—"I don't feel no ways tired"—echo a passage in the Bible. In Matthew 5:43–45, Jesus says, "You have heard that it was said, 'You shall love your neighbor and hate your enemy.' But I say to you, Love your enemies and pray for those who persecute you, so that you may be children of your Father in heaven; for he makes his sun rise on the evil and on the good, and sends rain on the righteous and on the unrighteous."

Is this not what Jesus Christ did when he carried his cross and died for us?

Truly, I am not an angry Black man. But I have to admit that at times I am bitter. I detest the vitriol spewed from the mouths of people who know nothing about me yet who find it suitable to declare that I don't belong here. That my life, and the lives of other people who look like me, are expendable. That what I have worked hard to achieve has been stolen from someone of another color who is more deserving. Why does the price paid for something we already have—something like freedom—cost so much?

One thing we could use more of in our country and around the world is faith—faith in humankind, faith in the unknown. When faith abounds, life becomes more meaningful. When we practice our faith, we believe our cries for human rights and social justice, even if they are loud and insistent, are the voices of reason echoing the words of people from every background across every spectrum. All God's children.

Slogans like "Hands up, don't shoot," or "Black Lives Matter," and "Stay woke" represent the gorgeous mosaic of colorful arms raised heavenward. The voices of "I Can't Breathe" belong to multicultural people speaking with a chorus of different accents, all of them gasping for the oxygen of fairness.

Our faith teaches us to hear the voices of our brothers and sisters who are begging for freedom, fairness, justice. The tragedy is that nobody should have to beg for these God-given rights. For starters, freedom is the American promise written into the Constitution of the United States. The reality is we must work together to ensure the rights of all people.

In 1967, singer and civil rights activist Nina Simone recorded "I Wish I Knew How It Would Feel to Be Free." In this song, Ms. Simone sang about the joy of liberation:

Well, I wish I could be like a bird in the sky
How sweet it would be if I found I could fly
Oh, I'd soar to the sun and look down at the sea. . . .
I'd know how it feels to be free.

Fifty-eight years after this song was recorded, Blacks and other marginalized people in the United States of America are still hoping for freedom in the full sense of the experience.

While we are called to care for the earth and to address the needs of the hungry, the unhoused, the sick, and the poor, I am reminded of Pope Francis's courageous declaration of 2016 as the Extraordinary Jubilee of Mercy (or the Year of Mercy). He instructed us to increase our responsiveness to caring for others. He reminded us to counsel the doubtful, instruct the ignorant, pray for sinners, comfort the afflicted, forgive offenses, bear wrongs with patience, pray for the living and the dead, and pray for the troubled and the troublemakers.

How hard can it be to care for others? Very, especially when we all have our own personal problems. If it were easy the pope would not have to ask, and neither would Andrew Young nor Dr. King have made careers out of asking. They are not asking us to administer care to every single person on earth—no one person is capable of doing that. What they are asking, and have demonstrated with their lives, is that, individually, we care for *someone*.

We've heard this message before. When will we actually heed the sage counsel to change the world by caring more? By reaching out? By doing instead of cowering?

Even into his nineties, Andrew Young continues to epitomize servant leadership. He lives his life committed to caring for the underserved. When he gets the call, he answers.

What is your call to action? Is it joining your community leaders and your local police force to develop solutions to police shootings? Is it participating in a local food bank to distribute food to the hungry? Is it volunteering your time to teach children of migrant workers how to read, write, and speak English? Is it helping people whose homes were burned to ashes during wildfires? Is it ministering to brokenhearted survivors of natural disasters who lost family members, companion animals, and personal possessions that will be gone forever?

How is your faith leading you toward the next good thing to do?

**This I know:**

Faith doesn't promise comfort, but it anchors us when life shakes the ground beneath our feet.

**Hold fast to dreams**

**For if dreams die**

**Life is a broken-winged bird**

**That cannot fly.**

LANGSTON HUGHES

## CHAPTER 8

# Dare to Dream

Dr. Martin Luther King, Jr. was assassinated on April 4, 1968. He was only thirty-nine years old; I was thirteen years old and preparing to graduate from St. Anthony of Padua Elementary School.

While in high school I learned more and more about Dr. King and the civil rights movement. In 1971, during my junior year in high school, I was selected to participate in the Archbishop's Leadership Project, a program started in 1967 to recruit young Black men into the priesthood. The concept was the brainchild of then-Auxiliary Bishop Terence Cooke (who would be named a cardinal in 1969) of New York. Cooke appointed Father John T. Meehan, a young Irish Catholic priest in Harlem, as coordinator of the program, and he recruited academically gifted Black students from Catholic high schools in New York City to participate in the program. The requirements for acceptance were having above average grades, demonstrating strong leadership capabilities, being highly respected by students and faculty, and surviving an intense interview process.

Early in the program things didn't go as planned. Following the death of Dr. King, the country was still immersed in the civil rights movement. The first cohort of young Black high school men called a meeting with Father Meehan to express concerns about the direction of the program. They believed there was a dire need for Black men to become leaders in other fields, more so than in the priesthood. Father Meehan took the idea back to Bishop Cooke, who agreed. With our input, Father Meehan shifted the program to create opportunities for us to expand our knowledge of Black history, civil rights, and social justice. We read books by Black authors, went to African American museums, attended Black theatrical productions on Broadway, and were taught the art of extemporaneous speaking. In short, we immersed ourselves in Black culture. In the five decades of the program, extraordinary men have gone through the Archbishop's Leadership

Project, including one who is now a Jesuit, Father Greg Chisholm. Many are doctors, lawyers, educators, scholars, entrepreneurs, and business and political leaders who do whatever we can to move Dr. King's dream forward.

Though my retirement years keep accumulating, Dr. King's words and actions continue to inspire me to volunteer my time in diversity, social justice, healthcare disparities, and community service projects. Three times during my career I've delivered a keynote speech to diverse audiences in unexpected venues on Dr. King's birthday. I've also had the privilege of assuming the podium in front of parents, young adults, community leaders, and business colleagues at a major healthcare company; parishioners of a Catholic church; and students and faculty at a private southern Christian university. In each instance, I would prepare by studying Dr. King's famous "I Have a Dream" speech, which he delivered on August 28, 1963, at the historic March on Washington for Jobs and Freedom rally. I would also read for inspiration his "Letter from Birmingham Jail," written in April 1963.

I feel blessed whenever I speak about the life of Dr. King. The opportunity allows me to understand my purpose as a diversity and social justice leader. When I look into the audience and meet the gaze of the people looking up at me and listening to my every word, I wonder whether they are hearing my voice speaking the words of Dr. King, or they are hearing the voice of Dr. King speaking through me? Are they connecting to the messages? Are my words enough to hold us accountable for advancing Dr. King's dream?

Throughout my life, whenever I say his name, I feel his presence and cannot help but wonder whether Dr. King is pleased with our progress in civil rights. I often wonder what the world would be like now if he were still alive. What would he think about the state of civil rights and social justice in our country and around the world? Would he be satisfied? I think not. While much work has been done to achieve a society free of injustice, we still have a long way to go. If he were here today, I think he would want us to join him in soothing the souls of the brokenhearted, the desolate ones who, even now, all these years later, yearn for justice.

In "The American Dream" speech delivered on Independence Day, July 4, 1965, Dr. King challenged America to imagine a place where, despite the scorching heat of civil unrest and regardless of the stormy torrents of racial disturbances, this nation could become an oasis of equal opportunity. His remarks align closely with what President Abraham Lincoln said on November 19, 1863, in his Gettysburg Address. In this speech, Lincoln beckoned America to never waiver from the journey of liberating the oppressed from the degrading chains of segregation. Dr. King's dream of a unified America was not popular during the civil rights period in America. Yet he never ceased in his efforts to fight for marginalized people. Dr. King worked to ensure—as President Franklin D. Roosevelt, who was paralyzed from the waist down, observed with a touch of irony—that we would not become a nation "paralyzed" by the insanity of injustice.

It is recorded in American history that Dr. King and President Lincoln both championed freedom and equality for all, though in different eras and with different approaches. Lincoln, as president, fought to preserve the Union and end slavery, while King advocated for civil rights and an end to racial discrimination through nonviolent resistance. Both drew inspiration from the ideals of the Declaration of Independence and the notion of a more perfect union. They were seminal leaders who bravely confronted the same problem: a divided America. They dedicated their lives to battling injustice and paid the ultimate price, which was to be struck down by the bullet of an assassin.

One of my favorite quotes by Dr. King is "The ultimate measure of a man is not where he stands in moments of comfort and convenience, but where he stands at times of challenge and controversy." This quote should be a reminder to us all to never give up hope in the pursuit of equal rights. Dr. King's faith in us serves to embolden us to continue working hard to make his dream a reality. In his actions he demonstrated what the true spirit of helping others means, even—or perhaps especially—when his own life was at risk, and his tireless, selfless efforts in support of human rights changed the course of history. It is true that one of his greatest gifts was his service to others. He certainly had the courage to say yes when his help was needed most. But the other great gift he shared with us was his faith. We must continue the work begun by Dr. King; as we do, we must emulate his courageous faith. We cannot afford to let *his* dream die. Come to think of it, his dream is—or should be—*our* dream. Dr. King, who imagined a world in which all God's children would live in harmony, will always be remembered as a brilliant man, a great orator, a civil rights giant, and a rare visionary. In another era, Dr. King would be considered a prophet.

What is our role in creating a better country, a better world, a place where goodwill toward every human being is the standard? We should not have to wait for turbulent times to act. What would Dr. King want us to do for the sick, the poor, the hungry, the frightened? Would he want us to be part of the problem or part of the solution? I think the answer is obvious.

**This I know:**

Dreaming boldly is not just ambition. It's faith in motion, especially when others doubt what you are seeing for yourself.

**The worst thing about the miracle of modern communications is the Pavlovian pressure it places upon everyone to communicate whenever a bell rings.**

RUSSELL BAKER

CHAPTER 9

# Honesty, Honor, Humility, and Humor

The late Russell Baker—author, *The New York Times* columnist, and two-time recipient of the Pulitzer Prize—was on the money when he coined the quote that introduces this chapter. How many times have we found ourselves responding to someone's question or statement when in reality they aren't expecting—and do not want—our response? News flash: I'm guilty of this! In fact, probably all of us are guilty of knee-jerk responses in situations where the speaker would prefer a listening ear over a talking mouth. Even so, how often does someone tell us that? How often do we let each other know, *Hey, thank you, but I'm not looking for a response. I just need you to listen.*

Lesson learned, courtesy of my first boss. When I entered the workforce as a manager in corporate communications with responsibilities for writing speeches for senior executives as well as being able to deliver speeches myself, my boss taught me how to remedy the awkward state of being hyperverbal. No matter the situation—I could be engaged in a one-on-one conversation or I could be delivering a speech to a crowd—there are three main rules to follow. First, speak to express, not to impress. Second, stay on point. And third, K.I.S.S. (Keep It Short and Simple).

Of my forty-year career, thirty years were spent working in communications in both the public and private sectors. Those sectors include, as I have shared, the healthcare industry. I also served as press secretary for a congressman and a mayor, which meant writing their speeches and at times delivering the speeches for them. I also worked as an advertising copywriter for a publishing company, a speech writer for senior pharmaceutical executives, and a freelance journalist for magazines and newspapers. In each of these roles, I had to practice the three main rules of communication, as well.

Writing is one of my passions. A blank screen on my desktop computer or an empty sheet of paper excites me.

I'm like a child digging into the stuffed toy chest, overjoyed about choosing whatever I want to play with. When I sit down to write, my mind is cluttered with thoughts and perspectives waiting to take shape; but then, one word leads to a sentence, then a paragraph, then a page. For me, there's more room to express myself on paper than in a conversation. It's akin to being immersed in a space that seems like a vault stored with valuable information waiting to be tapped into. In that space, I am freely engaged in self-reflection and exploration.

However, one of the most nerve-racking experiences is when I write speeches for other people to deliver. It's not the process of writing the speech that worries me; it's creating the right positioning for someone else that's tough. Speakers love when an audience is motivated after their speech is delivered, and most speakers hope to communicate a message that makes an impact. Some have different goals, like wanting to leave the audience spellbound, even though more important than having a spellbound experience is whether the audience walks away feeling that the speaker was honest and honorable. If the speaker also communicates sincere humility and a sense of humor, well then that's a good speaker delivering a fine speech.

I saw my role as speechwriter as helping the speaker reach what I call the Four H Principles of effective communication: *honesty*, *honor*, *humility*, and *humor*. The thing is, these four principles are guideposts for communicating effectively and should be kept in mind not only in the act of speechwriting but whenever we connect with one another.

This holds true in prayer as well. For example, when Wendy and I pray, normally, our prayers are serious. But sometimes something funny finds its way into our ritual, and when that happens we stop, open our eyes, look at each other, and burst out laughing. For example: *Dear God, thank you for giving me more blessings than Wendy today.* As if it's a competition. We hope at that moment God has a sense of humor. Prayer reflects our faith. It is how we communicate with God, and being honest and humble should be the way we honor Him.

Whenever I write a speech for someone, I schedule a meeting. The purpose is to find out what the person wants to say, but it's also an opportunity to get to know more about the person. Tell me about your background, your family. What was it like growing up? What do you like about being an executive? What makes you laugh? What is something about you the audience doesn't know? The point of this exercise is to know enough to position the speaker as authentic, approachable, and more than an anonymous corporate executive.

We've all been in the awkward situation of opening our mouths and saying something unintended and wishing we could take it back. However, public speaking doesn't work that way. It's not like fishing, when we put the bait on the hook and throw the hook and line into the water. If we make an undesirable catch, we can throw that fish back and give it another try. In public speaking, what we say cannot be unsaid. We don't get a do-over. Denzel uses this analogy about theater versus motion pictures: When an actor on a movie set recites something that isn't in the script, the director says, *Cut! Let's do it again,* but on the stage in front of a live audience, if an actor flubs a line, the director can't yell, *Cut!*

Honestly, honesty is easy. All we have to do is, well, be honest. We know when we're not being honest as soon as the words come off our lips. It's noticeable. When we start with honest communication, we connect. Most people pick up cues, and they can sense when we're pulling their leg. Audiences respond well to honesty, and the same dynamic is true during a one-on-one exchange. No one likes to be cheated. Regaining trust is not so easy.

For example, take the act of reconciliation, which I grew up calling confession. Reconciliation is one of the seven sacraments of the Catholic Church. With a priest listening attentively, reconciliation offers us an opportunity to cleanse ourselves of sins we committed. When we express our wrongdoings, our relationship with God is strengthened, renewed, and honest. We feel complete. We feel a sense of comfort. We are comforted because we cared enough to go through a whole process that involves being honest with God.

Along with honesty, communication also taps into honoring one another. Whenever someone asks about my faith, the answer is always, "I am *honored* to be Catholic." When we speak to audiences, one of the first things we should let them know is how honored we are to be in their presence. Their time and attention are valuable, not to be discounted. Know your audience so that you can express sincere respect for who they are, what they've done, where they've been, and whom they serve. Watch the expressions on the faces of veterans when they are thanked for their service. They feel honored. They feel connected.

Several years ago, I delivered a keynote speech at a Christian university in Tennessee at a celebration honoring Dr. King. The audience was predominantly White. While I was a little uncomfortable, I felt their kindness, their uplifting energy as they welcomed me with enthusiastic applause, and my nervousness abated. I delivered my remarks and received a standing ovation. (Phew!) A chain reaction spread through that auditorium, and in the end, it seems that we all felt honored.

There are two sides to communication. There's making a statement, about expressing what's in our minds and hearts. And there's asking a question so that we can learn something new. It takes humility to admit that we don't know something, and even more humility to then assume the role of listening to someone who knows more than we do.

Humility and humor go hand in hand. Humility creates a comfort zone and reveals our transparency while humor is the great equalizer. I once saw the chairman of the board of trustees of a university read his commencement remarks from his iPad to an audience of about three thousand people. A few minutes into the speech, he paused and started fiddling with the device. He looked up at the audience, looked down at his iPad, and belted out a resounding laugh right into the microphone that echoed around the campus. "I lost my place!" he said. Infectious laughter spread throughout the audience of students and guests. What a memorable moment that nobody there will ever forget! Humility and humor are valuable assets whenever we engage with family, friends, colleagues, or fellow students. When we laugh at our own foibles or miscues, we are being genuine. After all, we are human, which is to say that we are not perfect. Embrace who we are.

Communicating effectively is like playing chess in that we are more successful when we think before we act. So why does communication, whether speaking or writing, create so much agita? Managing effective communication starts with three simple questions: What is it we want to say? What's the best way to say it? And what do we intend to happen after it's been said?

Whether it's delivering a speech, making a presentation during a meeting, conducting a one-on-one performance review, pitching an idea about a new product, having a conversation with our significant other, chilling with our best friend, or talking with God in prayer, communication matters, and using these three guidelines will help us be better communicators.

Dale Carnegie, the great American writer and lecturer and developer of courses in self-improvement, salesmanship, corporate training, public speaking, and interpersonal skills, once said, "A talk is a voyage with a purpose, and it must be charted. The speaker who starts nowhere generally gets there." He was right, of course. It's up to us to decide where we want to go, whom we want by our sides during the journey, and how to stay connected with one another in authentically give-and-take, listen-and-respond, heart-to-heart relationships.

**This I know:**

Living well means telling the truth, walking with integrity, staying grounded, and never losing your ability to laugh.

**In my heart I hear music that has no words, harmony that has no sound: yet so gladsome is what I hear that nothing in the world can be compared thereto.**

ST. IGNATIUS OF LOYOLA

## CHAPTER 10

# A Love Affair with African Djembe Drums

I discovered my love of the African djembe drum in 1992 when I heard a song by the musical artist Vinx De'Jon Parrette, known professionally as Vinx. He is a singer, songwriter, and *djembefola* (one who plays djembe drums).

I am mesmerized by his music.

My favorite song, "Tell My Feet," is my go-to anthem for joy and jubilation when the weight of the world lies heavy on my shoulders. Every time I hear this song I am blown away. The lyrics are powerful and liberating, and they let me find clarity in the importance of living an abundant life on earth with generosity, service to humankind, and love for all God's creations. Vinx sings,

If I could walk along the shores and hear the ocean
whispering once more
A voice so clear to those who hear so blind
Could I believe what my heart knew all along
Tell my feet I made it home. I made it home.

I believe the lyrics are telling us to listen and reflect on God's goodness, and urging us to prepare ourselves for the ultimate gift of going Home to where He's been waiting for us. I'm not certain this is the interpretation Vinx intended, but the power of his words and their alignment to my faith allow this song to set my soul on fire.

Vinx's smooth, melodic, and soothing voice joins in perfect harmony with the African rhythms he pounds out on his drums. He sings while playing two, sometimes three, djembe drums. Playing one djembe drum is difficult all by itself because there are three sounds involved. The first is the *bass*, which is the result of opening the hand with all the fingers joined together and hitting the center of the drum with the palm of your hand. The second is the *smack*, which creates a crisp, flat sound by separating your fingers as you strike on the right or left side of the drumhead. And the third is the *tone*, which involves using only the fingers to hit around the rim of the drumhead. When each of the sounds comes together you hear the fullness of the drum.

How do I know this? I am a djembefola, too. I learned to play these drums (also known as talking drums) at the age of ten. An older man who lived in my neighborhood in the South Bronx had studied African drumming, and he was kind enough to hand down all that he knew about this tradition. To this day, I enjoy every opportunity to play my djembe drums, especially on Wednesday nights when I join thirty to forty drummers in an outdoor drum circle in Florida. We come together with a shared passion for making music. It's that simple.

To me, the drum circle is a reminder of the power of diversity. In the circle there are people of all ages from very different backgrounds—some Black, some White, some Latino, some highly skilled, and some beginners. We hang out together for three hours. There is no tension. No judgment about who plays better than the other. Each of us joins together to create a wonderful display of multiculturalism at its finest. We drum ourselves into oblivion, all of us sharing the same single-minded objective of making music.

African drumming is hypnotic, something that can be an out-of-body experience. I improvise staccato rhythms as other drummers are simultaneously creating unrehearsed beats. Strangely, it sounds harmonized. When I hear talking drums I think about my purpose on earth as a Black man. As a husband, father, grandfather. As a retired senior officer in corporate America who led diversity. And as a Catholic. When I am participating in the circle, I know I matter. My rhythms matter. My improvisations matter. What my talking drum says matters. And in this communal call-and-answer where we bring our entire essence into the conversation—conversation involving drumheads, hands, hearts, personal histories, and minds—I feel that I am more than enough.

Drumming is powerful. It's magnetic and inviting. It soothes our pain. It erases our anxieties. In the drum circle no one fights. No one talks politics. No one's faith is questioned. We just play drums.

How is it that a drum circle can bring together an array of people from different backgrounds and create the kind of cooperative effort the 106th Mayor of New York City, David Dinkins, who, in 1989, was the first African American to serve as mayor of New York City, referred to as "the gorgeous mosaic of God's creations"? It happens because while the drums are playing, we release our hearts and souls unabashedly, without fear of judgement. Each drummer has a different beat. Each dancer moves their body uniquely.

Oh yes—one more thing—women, men, and children run to the center of the circle and dance to the rhythms while I smack my drums to accentuate the movement of their bodies. The team play between the drummers and dancers is liberating. Exhilarating.

When I am playing my djembe drum, I am also keenly listening and paying close attention to the rhythms of the other drummers. I am constantly seeking opportunities to blend the beats that I hear in my own mind with the rhythms they are putting out into our collective energy. With my ears I search for the disruptions and the offbeats. When I find them, I insert my own message into those openings. This is when the drums really start talking to one another. To the uninitiated, the pitter-patter of talking drums may sound a bit chaotic. In many ways, like the sound of a group of excited teenagers chattering as they climb aboard a field-trip bus, it is. I call it rhymical chaos as created by a diverse set of people from all backgrounds and highlighting the beauty of diversity. I think to myself, *This is where we can find God.* With so much stuff going on in the world today that prevents us from talking with one another, listening to talking drums lets us hear the joy and pain carried by our brothers and sisters.

Drumming begs the questions, *How do we find hope in the pitter-patter? Are our drums the voices of the voiceless?* Or are there better questions? *Can our drums speak for the ones whose voices are not heard? Does our drumming make us better listeners, better able to be the voices of those who have been silenced?*

When I was a young boy learning to play the djembe drum, I didn't know then what I know now: Drumming is a metaphor for communication, delivered with an overlay of unspoken messages. The key to a good life is living in community with people who have shared values, such as those you find in a drum circle. No one should ever be permitted to cast someone aside because of the color of their skin, or the accent of their voice, or the beat of their drum. Each of us is a heartbeat seeking to fine-tune our existence. When this occurs, we are in harmony. We are connected even with our syncopated, disruptive, yet melodious sounds. As Janet Jackson sings, "We are a part of the rhythm nation."

A drum circle . . . a family circle . . . an extended family circle . . . the circle of life . . . is where we find God. I believe this is where we all want to be: at the center, with God. Unequivocally, I know for sure that I do.

**This I know:**

Joy lives in the rhythms of your soul,
and honoring your roots through your passions
keeps that joy alive.

**If you can't fly, then run.**

**If you can't run, then walk.**

**If you can't walk, then crawl,**

**but by all means, keep moving.**

MARTIN LUTHER KING, JR.

## CHAPTER 11

# Final Thoughts

When I woke up on the morning of November 6, 2024, I grabbed my cell phone and glanced at the headlines. I was in shock and disbelief. I looked over to see if Wendy was awake. She typically greets me with a beaming smile, giving me assurance that she slept well. This morning, however, she did not have a smile on her face. She had a question: "Who won?" "Not our candidate," I answered. She turned over in disbelief and said nothing else. At that moment, I reflexively thanked God for giving us a new day. Then I went into silent mode as well.

Slowly, gradually, Wendy and I began to share our thoughts of what the next four years might look like. We thought about our young adult children and our grandson and how they would be impacted. The one thing we both agreed upon was to never stop praying and never lose our faith in God. God is good all time and all the time God is good. He is loving and kind. In that spirit, as we have been doing for years, we will continue to reach out and help those who are in need regardless of the color of their skin or where they're from or what language they speak. We will keep our family and friends close and always be thankful for God's blessings.

One prayer stayed in my head throughout the day: *Lord, help me to know what you want, to want what you want, and to do what you want.* I prayed for guidance and grace in tempering my disappointment and fears about the outcome of the presidential election. And, since I believe service to humankind is the mandate of our existence and the price we pay for breathing God's air, I asked for God's help and instruction in guiding me to be of support and service to other people in shocked disbelief.

We live in a world where all God's children matter. A world in which diversity is our strength. My passion for diversity remains strong in spite of who is or is not elected president of the United States. I've seen the power diversity has in creating unity. However, it's discouraging when diversity is misconstrued as something that creates division. Diversity and division are polar opposites. We are all

God's creation, and that's irrefutable. Diversity will continue to be unsettling *until we are able to wrap ourselves around the fact that diversity is who we are.* I've met people who believe the concept of diversity robs them of their individuality, their uniqueness. This, despite the truth that we are all different—and yet, in so many ways, we are all the same. Diversity is what humanity exemplifies. The color of our skin, the power of our faith, and the uniqueness of our character are strengths that we bring to the work of building a better future for our children. Diversity is to be celebrated—not ridiculed, feared, erased, or eradicated. If anything, it should be emphasized because it's what enables us to appreciate our differences and similarities.

We exist in a multiethnic, multiracial world. Diversity is the personification of how all God's human creations work, live, and play together. A lack of diversity creates disharmony. Disharmony within one culture creates disharmony within all cultures. To achieve true harmony, we must have faith in humankind. Our future depends on it.

Questions to self: When you were a young child, what didn't you see that you see now? Would I have a best friend who is a world renowned celebrity—a friendship brought to me by none other than God? Would I have to dig deeply to figure out how to father my children because my own father passed away when I was seven? I didn't know how to be a father and thought I'd never learn. But I figured it out. I know that putting my children first was the toughest thing I ever tackled, yet the most rewarding. And being loved by them represents life's highest achievement. Did I allow a divorce to submerge me in a sea of emptiness? Yes, I did. But being graced with the presence of an angel helped me to revive my neglected connection to God and embrace the realization of true unconditional love. It was the WOW factor that reminded me about living with my ears peeled to the gentle suggestions given to me by God, instructing me to keep the communication lines going through prayer.

It helps me in my life when I remember that whether a president, emperor, king, or queen sits at the throne, only God wears the crown.

**This I know:**

If you live with love, purpose, and faith, your story can light the way for someone else.

Each of us is a heartbeat

seeking to fine-tune our existence.

When we do this—

even despite our syncopated, disruptive,

uniquely melodious sounds—

we are in harmony.

# Acknowledgments

To Wendy, who is absolutely my most precious gift from God: You found me when I was brokenhearted and your love lifted me up and renewed my existence. Each morning when I open my eyes, yours is the first smile I see. Whenever I need encouragement, you touch my index finger with yours and we point towards heaven, affirming that both you and God got me. Thank you for your love and for keeping me focused throughout this book-writing journey. To our children, Austin, Ashley, and Dayne, and to our grandson, Elijah: You enable me to live my best life. Over the years, I have been the beneficiary of your kind and loving ways. Each of you has made me a better human being. I love you beyond forever.

To my parents, Wendy's parents, and my godmother, who have all gone Home to heaven: You watched from above as I wrote this book. I felt your encouragement all the way through.

To my family and extended family: Thank you for your love, kindness, and encouragement. I'm blessed to have you all in my life. We are connected because of God's deliberate involvement.

To Denzel: When I asked you to write the foreword for my book, even without giving you much detail, you immediately answered yes. Your trust in me will always be one of the greatest treasures of my life. I am blessed to know you and Pauletta and the amazing family you two brought into this world.

To my editors: Gary Jansen, thank you for reading the very first draft of my work and seeing something intriguing enough to shape it into a collection of life stories. I am astonished at how our passion for Vinx and the djembe drum are shared experiences that brought us together. Maura Poston, you are incredible. You are more than an editor. I marvel at your ability to help me find my inner soul and push me deeper into it. You were my guiding light throughout the entire process, helping me to open my heart and share it unconditionally. I have grown immensely as a writer with your keen ability as my editor. You enabled me to put the awe into every story.

To my mentors: Randy Cameron, Jon Weisberg, Bill Nielsen, and John Doorley, you taught me how to navigate the ins and outs, the ups and downs of corporate America. Each of you empowered me to become an effective and confident communicator. You made my professional experience fulfilling.

To my fraternal brothers: Douglas Young and Shelley Stewart, Jr., you are published authors and accomplished men of character. Your gentle prodding and asking, "How's the book going, Doc?" kept me focused. I am honored to be in your company.

To my mentees: You know who you are. You have afforded me the privilege of being in your lives and have inspired me immensely.

To my Prospect Avenue brothers: Cameron Brome (RIP), Dr. Leon Rogers, Jr., Bob Harris, Wayne Clark, Solomon Land, Gerald McMillan, and David Parham, we are truly blessed to share a friendship immersed in brotherly love for more than sixty years. In every one of our Zoom meetings during the past six years each of you always asked, "Are you still working on that book?" Here it is!

To my dear friend David Benitah, who, after reading a poem I wrote during the COVID-19 pandemic, was so touched that you made me promise to write a book: I honored your instruction. I will always remember our rich conversations about Judaism and Catholicism, the Holocaust and the civil rights movement, and the power of faith. May you rest in peace.

To Fordham University, my beloved alma mater: You have poured into me so much of who I am. I am thankful.

# About the Author

Anthony P. Carter is a retired corporate executive, award-winning diversity strategist, and lifelong Catholic whose inspiring journey from the South Bronx to the C-suite has been shaped by faith, friendship, and commitment to service. A devoted husband, father, and grandfather, he continues to mentor, volunteer, and share stories that uplift and unite—and to work with tenacity and diligence on lowering his golf handicap.